Texas Jack's Famous Apple Cider Recipes

How to Make Sweet and Hard Cider. Recipes for Smoothies, Sweet Cider Punch, and Hot Sweet Cider Drinks

Dennis Waller

Disclaimer- This here book is for entertainment purposes only. Now, if you get a hankering to go out and turn into a Moonshiner based on what you learn in this book, well, I guess that's your business. But if a Revenuer like Eliot Ness comes a calling with a big old ax and a warrant, you're on your own and don't be going and implicating me any as the head honcho or ringleader. Causing if you do, well, I'll just have to remind you that I didn't tell you to do anything, other than enjoy this here book. But, if you do make up a batch that is downright good, I would be obliged to have a taste or two. Now that we have all the legal stuff out of the way, let's get busy with making some hard cider that even President John Adams would be proud of.

Copyright © 2014 Dennis Waller

All rights reserved.

ISBN: 1500604097
ISBN-13: 978-1500604097

DEDICATION

This is for Foghorn Leghorn for his commitment in advancing my education in the field of philosophy, weed pulling, glass blowing and cider making

CONTENTS

	Acknowledgments	i
1	Apple Cider	1
2	How to Make Sweet Cider	3
3	How to Make Hard Apple Cider	9
4	Hot Sweet Apple Cider Recipes	25
5	Sweet Apple Cider Smoothies	33
6	Cold Sweet Apple Cider Drinks	51
7	Other Texas Jack Recipe Books	59
8	A Brief History of the Original Texas Jack	65
9	About Dennis Waller	69

ACKNOWLEDGMENTS

I wish to thank Samuel Adams and their line of Angry Orchard Hard Apple Cider for inspiring me to learn how to make my own and to President John Adams for touting the greatness of drinking a healthy tankard of hard apple cider.

CHAPTER ONE
APPLE CIDER- AN INTRODUCTION

Apple cider and the making of apple cider are as much of our American Heritage as baseball and apple pie. Wow, seems these apples play an important part of our history, eh? Interestingly enough, President John Adams on just about every day of his adult life, started it off with a tankard of apple cider. When asked, his reply was, "To do me good." Must have been something to it as he lived to be 91 years old. Now to be clear here, drinking apple cider every day may or may not add to your longevity, but either way, it will certainly make life more enjoyable.

A side note of interest concerning President Adams and cider, in 1979 a federal regulation was put in place allowing citizens to produce all the hard cider they wanted. Of course, they meant it for home consumption only. So, don't go getting any ideas of becoming a "Moonshiner" as we wouldn't want anyone to break any laws as selling these types of alcoholic beverages is illegal. However, I didn't see anything about giving it away there, did you?

Just about anyone can make apple cider. Even though we can run down to the local store and pick up a bottle of apple cider, there is nothing more fun than making your own. It can be a fun way for a family to spend an afternoon. Going to the market and picking out a variety of apples and pressing them into cider is not only a rewarding experience but tasteful one too. Another great thing about apple cider is it can be enjoyed in the heat of summer chilled or around the fireplace in the depth of winter in a steaming hot mug with a cinnamon stick.

CHAPTER TWO
HOW TO MAKE SWEET CIDER

Selecting the Apples. For a gallon of fresh sweet cider you will need 16 pounds of apples. This can vary depending on the variety and mixture of apples used. Some varieties of apples have more juice than others. To be on the safe side, go with 16 pounds. If you do end up with more than a gallon of cider, then consider it a bonus.

When making cider I recommend using a mixture of different apples. A blend of three or more varieties is best in making sweet cider. A traditional mixture is one-third each of sweet, bittersweet and sharp apples. The complexity of the different flavors mixed together creates a more full bodied cider. But then again, it is always a personal preference and there is nothing wrong in making a batch of cider using nothing more than Granny Smith apples. As for me, I try to use as many different apples as possible. I enjoy experimenting with blending different varieties to see what wonderful flavors I can create and you should too. The point of all of this is to have fun.

If you are picking apples from your own orchard or sneaking into someone else's orchard,(I don't recommend this unless you have permission) make sure to pick quality apples. You don't want any bruised, wormy, or overripe apples. Windfalls, (those are apples that have fallen to the ground on their own) are fine to use as long as they not bruised or damaged. Here is a rule of thumb you can use- Would you eat it? If not, then don't use it for your cider.

For those who do not have apple trees growing nearby, the market is your best bet. I like going to a top tiered grocery store like Central Market, Whole Foods, or Market Street. The selection of apples offered is superb and it gives you the opportunity to try out new and different varieties of apples.

The equipment- Back in the day, apple cider was made at home with the use of a cider press. While cider presses are still available today, they can be expensive. Midwest Supplies has a nifty little press that would be perfect for making cider. It is the 25 pound Italian-Made Ratchet Wine Press and it sells for around $320.00. You can check it out at http://www.midwestsupplies.com/25-italian-made-ratchet-press.html

Time to Make some Sweet Cider

Wash the apples thoroughly. If the apples came from any other place than an organic farm, remove the stems and the end of the blossom, (that is the bottom of the apple) Chop up the apples into manageable pieces for the equipment you are using. Refer to the manufacturers guide as to what your device can handle and prepare the apples accordingly.

To make cider with a cider press, chop up the apples into small pieces, the smaller the better. Place the chopped apples into a large strainer or piece of cheesecloth. Some folks even use a pillow case, but I prefer a strainer. I use a 5 gallon paint strainer. You can get these from any paint or home improvement store. Like everything else we use, make sure it is sanitized.

Place the bag of chopped apples into the press. Apply pressure and wait until most of the juice has slowed to a trickle and then apply more pressure. This is a part of the process that you do not want to hurry. Let the laws of physics work for you and the pressure and gravity will do the job. Have patience my grasshopper and you'll be rewarded with sweet, fresh cider.

Take the cider you've collected from the press and pour it through a filter to remover anything that doesn't belong in there. You can use a large sieve and pour it directly into a large saucepan to pasteurize. If you want a clearer cider, you can add a coffee filter to the sieve but keep in mind it might take some time for the cider to filter through.

For those who do not have a cider press, it's okay. You can use a food processor, a blender, or a juicer. If you don't have a cider press, the next best thing is a juicer. This is the quickest method to use in separating the cider from the apples. Whatever you use, ensure to chop the apples to the right size for the device.

To pasteurize, place the sweet cider in a large saucepan and simmer over low heat at 160 to 180 degrees for 45 minutes. Be careful not to allow the cider to boil. Boiling the cider will cause pectins to set in and your cider will have a hazy appearance. Once the sweet cider has simmered, remove from the heat. Allow to cool to room temperature then refrigerate the cider immediately. At this stage, the sweet cider is ready.

Tips and Ideas

Why do I need to refrigerate the cider after pasteurizing it?

The flavor of cider starts maturing immediately. If the cider is left out at room temperature, it will begin to change from a sweet and tangy cider to a more mellow and fruity cider. In time the flavor will continue to change until it turns into vinegar. Refrigerated, cider will last for several weeks while maintaining its freshness and flavor. Cider can also be frozen and be kept for up to a year with the same results.

Can you tell me more about the different types of apples?

Apple cider producers use a blend of different apples to create a more desirable tasting cider. You want to use a balance of sweet apples and tart apples. However, there are times when you can only use what is available. This is an area that you can play with in coming up with your own blend of apples to create a flavorful cider that meets your taste. To give you a rundown of a few varieties, I have listed below the five most popular apples that can be found just about everywhere. But between you and me, my favorite is a variety called "**Pink Lady**" Well, it is by far, the best, most sweetest apple I have ever had and you know I always have a few in my cider.

•**Red Delicious**: Large, firm red apple with a sweet flavor. The standard for apples

•**Yellow Delicious**: Large, semi-firm yellow apple with a sweet flavor.

•**Gala**: Medium, crisp semi tart apple with skin blushed from yellow to orange to red tinge.

•**Jonathan**: Medium, crisp semi tart apple, with red at the top turning to green towards the bottom of the fruit.

•**Granny Smith**: Medium/small, very crisp, tart apple with bright green color. Great for baking

What is the difference between apple cider and apple juice?

Here in the United States the difference between apple cider and apple juice is cider is unfiltered apple juice that still contains some pulp and appears cloudy. Apple juice is filtered and appears clear. Outside the States, apple cider is the alcoholic version of what we call hard cider.

CHAPTER THREE
HOW TO MAKE HARD APPLE CIDER

The best cider to use in making hard cider is fresh sweet apple cider that you made yourself or bought from a local market. Fresh sweet cider has not been pasteurized nor does it contain any chemical preservatives.

Store bought apple cider that contains these chemical preservatives like sodium benzoate or potassium sorbate will kill the yeast and not allow for fermenting. However, if you use store bought apple cider, just ensure it is organic and doesn't contain any preservatives. A couple of my favorite retail ciders are Whole Foods "365 Organic" brand and "R.W. Knudsen." The best part, they both come in a Glass gallon jug therefore saving you money since you already have the container to make your hard cider in. If you find a different brand, read the label to ensure that the juice is natural and contains no preservatives.

Note- If you are using your own fresh sweet apple cider, you'll need to pasteurize it before using. No worries, this is a simple step. Place the sweet cider in a large saucepan and simmer over low heat at 160 to 180 degrees for 45 minutes. Be careful not to allow the cider to boil. Boiling the cider will cause pectins to set in and your cider will have a hazy appearance. Once the sweet cider has simmered, remove from the heat and allow to cool to room temperature. At this stage, the sweet cider is ready. This process aids in killing off any wild yeast, microorganisms or bacterial that could affect the results of your hard cider.

A little about Yeast- There are a variety of dry yeast available online and at homebrew stores. There are even specialized yeast packs in a liquid form just for making hard cider. However, you'll find that dry yeast are much less expensive and get the job done as well. I would encourage you to experiment with different types of yeast but to begin with we'll use Champagne Yeast, but a Sweet Mead Yeast is a good choice too.

Note- Lalvin E-1118: Comes in a 5g packet and cost less than a dollar. This is a wine/champagne yeast but it is also one of the most widely used yeasts in the world for "general application" like sparkling cider. It is a very vigorous yeast. This yeast goes fast. It will eat up all the sugar you give it and stop when it is dry. Then it will carbonate up fast. This is a good choice to start with.

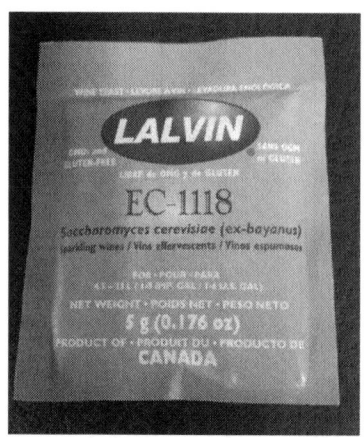

Fermentation Locks- These are readily available and very inexpensive. The purpose of a fermentation lock is to allow the gases to escape and to keep microbes and critters like gnats and flies out. A traditional lock has two chambers filled with water; this enables the gasses to escape while providing a secure seal for the cider. The lock fits into a rubber stopper that fits into the top of the bottle.

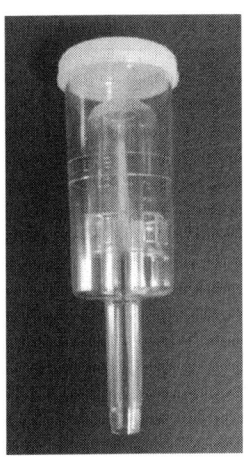

However, you can make your own with something as simple as a balloon. If you decide to go old-school and use a balloon over a conventional fermentation lock, there are a few things you should know. When using a balloon, just make sure the balloon is secured on the bottle. This can be done by tying it down with a string, a rubber band, or with tape. Either way, you don't want the balloon flying off, so make sure it is on there to stay. Next, it is necessary to put a pinhole in the balloon to allow the gases to escape. If you use this method, I would recommend keeping an eye on the balloon, just to make sure everything stays to plan.

The Equipment- This is what makes this so much fun to do, it doesn't require a lot and can be done for less than ten dollars. Now as far as a jug, I highly recommend using a glass gallon jug. Some folks say it's fine to use plastic and even the homebrew shops sell plastic brew buckets. But for me, it is a glass gallon jug. Earlier I stated that I prefer using 365 Organic or R.W. Knudsen for the fact that the quality of the cider is as good as you can get but also for the handy jug it comes in.

For those who are unable to find these two brands: here are a couple of suggestions for getting a glass jug. One is to buy a "demijohn" or "carboy" bottle. These are bottles that come in a variety of sizes and will serve the purpose. They are available at homebrew stores and some retail stores.

Another bottle that works great are the Carlos Russo one gallon wine bottles. I have known folks that have bought the wine and poured it out just to use the bottle. If you are creative I am sure you can rustle one up for next to nothing. Either way, just get you a glass gallon jug and we're ready.

Once your hard cider is ready to bottle, also known as racking, you'll need something to put it in. Well, there are a couple of ways of doing this. I prefer using plastic soda pop bottles that we save. They are sturdy and the caps stay on. They were designed to be used for carbonated beverages. Some folks use water bottles but I have found them to be just a tab too flimsy. For a one-gallon batch of hard cider, all you need is eight to ten 16 ounce bottles. Whatever you use, just make sure they have been sanitized. We'll get to that next.

Keep it Clean! Sanitizing- If you're using 365 Organic or R.W. Knudsen apple cider in their bottle, then you're good. If not, then we need to get your fermentation bottle clean as well as everything you'll be using. First off, give everything a good cleaning by washing it, either in the sink or in a dishwasher, that includes the fermentation lock, stopper, glass jug, and whatever else you plan on using. You can do this process for the plastic bottles once you're ready to rack your hard cider.

Next step is to sanitize your equipment. This can be done by using a quality sanitizer like "Iodophor" or "Star San" which are available at just about any homebrew supply store or online. If you are unable to locate these, another option is using bleach like "Clorox." Fill up the sink and measure out the desired amount of sanitizer, which is usually is about one tablespoon per five gallons of water. For beach, it is one tablespoon per one gallon of water.

Submerged the items and let soak for at least 20 minutes. For the gallon jug, if it doesn't fit in the sink, simply fill it up to the top and let it soak. After soaking, I like to pour out the sanitizing solution and rinse with boiling water. Now, this is where you need to be extremity careful in not getting hurt. With the smaller items, you can give them a rinse by dipping them in a pot of boiling water and allowing them to air dry. With the gallon jug, pour some boiling water in there and give it a good swirl and pour it out, allowing it to air dry. The purpose of this is to ensure we get rid of any residue of the beach or sanitizer. Plus it goes a long way in getting all those nasty bacterial and microbes deader than dead.

It's Time to make some Hard Cider

The moment we all have been waiting for! Yep, it is time to get busy making some hard cider. By now we have some sweet cider to use. If it is fresh cider, we have already pasteurized it by simmering it on the stove and allowing it to cool off, or we are using store bought cider like R.W. Knudsen. If we are using the R.W. Knudsen or similar brand, pour out about four to six ounces of cider. Either way, you want the jug about 9 tenths full.

Note- Here is a trick to increase the alcohol content to your hard cider. Before adding the yeast, pour out about a quart of the cider into a saucepan. Over low heat add 2 cups of packed light brown sugar. Stir until completely dissolved and let it simmer for 15 minutes. Remove from heat and allow to cool to room temperature. Then pour back into the gallon jug. Now, you're back on track.

Take the yeast and measure out the required amount in a sterilized cup. Most packs of yeast are for five gallon batches, so you really don't want to use the entire pack. A quarter of the pack will do just fine. Don't worry if you get a little too much yeast, it isn't going to hurt anything. Now add about 2 ounces of warm water to the yeast and give it a good swirl to get the yeast dissolved. Once thoroughly mixed add the yeast mixture to the cider. Place the cap back on the jug and give it a good swirl to get the yeast mixed in with the cider. Remove the cap and install your fermentation lock. Place the jug in a cool dark place and let the yeast go to work. Some folks like to keep it in a closet or in the laundry room. I like to keep mine on the kitchen counter with a brown paper bag over it. Whatever you do, keep it out of direct sunlight and someplace cool, at least 75 degrees or less.

Let the cider set and ferment for 5 days. Yes, it is okay to take a peek at it to make sure the fermentation lock is working and to check on the progress of the bubbling. Within 24 hours it should be going to town with all the bubbling going on. Now the fermenting time will depend on your own personal taste. I like a sweeter hard cider so I cut my fermenting time to 5 days. For a drier less sweet hard cider, you can let it ferment longer. You can go for up to two weeks or until the bubbling subsides.

After the desired time has pass, it is time to bottle it. Having your sanitized bottles and funnel ready, be careful to pour the cider as to not disturb the settlement on the bottom of the jug. Fill each bottle to about 9 tenths full.

Now, if you want to carbonate your hard cider, add a half teaspoon of Corn Sugar. Corn Sugar is readily available at any homebrew store or online. You can buy a ¾ cup of corn sugar on Amazon for less than two dollars plus shipping. It is critical to use corn sugar to get the carbonation right. After placing the corn sugar in the bottle of cider, screw on the top tightly and give it a slight swirl to help the corn sugar dissolve. Another product you can use and makes the process a little easier is called Coopers Carbonation Drops. It is a sugar in a drop form. One tablet per 12 ounce bottle will do the trick. They are available at your local homebrew store and online.

Place the bottles back in a cool dark place and allow to age. For someone like me, I can't wait. I'll give it a day or two, once the bottle feels hard like it did when it contained soda, then I'll place it in the fridge for another day or two before drinking it.

Tips and Ideas

How long to let it age?

Now, believe it or not, hard cider does get better as it ages. The apple flavor becomes more distinct with age. You can give it a taste once a week to see where the flavor is. If you hit on a time where the hard cider is just right, make sure to note how long you let it aged for next time. As far as aging goes, it is a personal preference. The best way to learn is through trial and error.

Why add sugar?

Some recipes out there call for adding sugar. The purpose of adding sugar is to increase the alcohol content. Some use honey, others agave syrup. It doesn't really matter as again the end game is to increase the alcohol content by adding food for the yeast to eat so it can convert into alcohol. Remember, the more sugar you add, the more alcohol you will get. With the sugar, it will increase the time to ferment. And try not to use more than 2 cups per gallon of cider, we want to make a delicious drink, not rocket fuel.

If want to get all fancy you can get a Hydrometer. This is a device that measures the amount of sugar in the cider used to determine the specific gravity and the potential alcohol content of the cider. The more sugar in the cider, the heavier it is. The hydrometer will give you the information needed to compute the percentage of alcohol. Most hard ciders are in line with beer and wine on alcohol content. This is an area that is up to the brewer as to their individual taste. For those interested in taking the game to the next level, go out and get yourself one of these hydrometers. Read the instructions so you can get all scientific. As for me, I'll just drink it the way it is.

I really want a Strong Cider, how do I do that?

Applejack is a cider that has an alcohol content way above what can be done by fermenting. There are two ways to achieve this. One is through distilling it. However, there are government regulations to contend with since they don't look too favorably on someone running a still. At that point, you're set up to make moonshine, which isn't a bad thing I guess but those folks up there in Washington take a dim view on it. So with that said, let's take a look at the second method.

You can achieve the same results by simply freezing the hard cider. In a large pot, one that gives you a large surface area, pour your cider into it and place in the freezer. Slushy ice will form on the top, which is the water in the cider freezing. Remove the ice. By reducing the water content, you automatically increase the alcohol content. It is not uncommon to achieve a cider with a 40% alcohol content using this method. And, the best part, it keeps the revenuers away.

I want my hard cider sweeter without adding to the alcohol content

Well, there is an answer for that too. When you go to bottle your hard cider, give it a taste. If you would prefer a sweeter cider, then add a sweetener that the yeast will not eat. My choice for this task is Stevia. You can also use Splenda but I like keeping it natural so I use Stevia which a sweetener and sugar substitute made from the leaves of the Stevia plant. Just look up Splenda on Wikipedia and you'll find that there are a whole lot of words that just don't sound too appealing like maltodextrin. Keep it as organic and natural as possible. Remember back in the days of John Adams, I highly doubt they were using any of this non-sense.

I want my cider to have a stronger apple flavor

This can be done but it requires that you cheat a little. The best way to improve on the apple flavor in your hard cider is to add frozen apple juice concentrate to the sweet cider. Make sure you do this step before adding the yeast. If you go this route, allow the frozen apple juice concentrate to thaw before using. Pour out 4 ounces of sweet cider from the jug. Measure 4 ounces of the apple juice concentrate and pour into the gallon jug. Place the cap back on the jug and give it a good swirl to mix the concentrate and sweet cider. You're now ready to add the yeast mixture.

I want my hard cider to be clear as the driven snow

Well, that's okay and guess what? Yep, there is something for that, it's called Pectic Enzyme. The purpose of using a pectic enzyme is to reduce the hazing effects during the fermentation process. There are several pectic enzymes on the market and readily available at your homebrew store or online. The directions vary little but most call for ¾ teaspoon per gallon of cider and you add in at the time you add the yeast. No worries as the pectic enzyme will not affect the taste of the finished hard cider, so it is a personal choice.

Is there another way to pasteurize fresh sweet cider prior to making hard cider?

There are three main methods used in pasteurizing sweet cider for use in making hard cider. Two of which you can do at home. The first and my favorite method is heating up the cider and allowing the heat to kill off any wild yeast along with anything else that might be in there that you don't want.

The second method and one that I don't care for, involves using an item called Campden Tablets. Campden tablets are also known as potassium or sodium metabisulfite. Well, that is enough for me not wanting to use it. If I can't spell or say it, I don't want it in my food or drink. However, for the sake of furthering our education into the science of Hard-Cider Making, we'll take a look at it. Campden tablets are a sulfur-based product that is used primarily in wine, cider and beer making to kill bacteria and to inhibit the growth of most wild yeast. If you make any type of juice from fresh fruits, then no matter what, there will be wild yeast in it.

The big boys use a process called "cold pasteurization." Now, this is a process that exposes the juice to low level gamma rays. Yep, that's right, X-Rays. Or sometimes they will use an electron beam. These rays and beams are used to reduce or kill microorganisms, such as e-coli, listeria, salmonella and campylobacter that may cause illnesses from exposure to these harmful pathogens. Sounds like something right out of a Buck Rogers episode. I don't know about you, but that there stovetop method makes the most sense to me in getting my fresh cider pasteurized. I don't really care for x-rays or sodium metabisulfite. Remember what grandma use to say, "Keep it simple." Letting the sweet cider simmer on the stovetop is your best bet for pasteurizing.

I want to add a little something to flavor it up

There are some folks out there that would like to have a cinnamon taste to their hard cider or a spiced flavor. Well, after talking to the folks that have been down that road, here are their thoughts. If it is a solid like a spice, such as a cinnamon stick or a dose of spices like allspice or nutmeg, then add after the fermentation has stopped. You can add it to the cider when you bottle it, to give it time to infuse the cider. If you place these spices in the cider during the fermentation, there is a strong possibility the spices will corrupt the cider giving a gad awful taste. So, add any spices after the fermentation has stopped, okay?

Now, for liquids, let's say you want a mango taste mixed in with your cider. This is easy to accomplish. R.W. Knudsen among others has an extensive line of organic non-preservative juices you can use. R.W. Knudsen has a wonderful mango juice, along with several other flavors. Pick the flavor you would like and add to your cider.

Here is the best method to making your own concoction of devilishly delightful hard cider. Before you add the yeast, pour out whatever amount of apple cider you desire to have replaced with the juice of your choice. Pour in the new juice to make up the difference. It is that simple. However, there are a few things you need to know. If you use a cherry cider or a grape juice, this will affect the fermentation time. Instead of 5 days, it might be 4 days. A good way to check on it is to keep an eye on the bubbling but the best test is to taste it. If you allow the cider with the grapes to go too long, the grape juice will develop a sour taste in the cider rather quickly. It is one of those things that you just need to monitor if you are going to experiment with blending juices.

In fact, there is no rule that says you have to use apple cider. You can use any juice you want. The basics are the same, whether it is apple cider or pineapple juice. But let's try to figure this out with apple cider before going off in a different direction. However, I do encourage you to try out new things and experiment because that is how you learn and master the craft of home brewing. But for the sake of this book, let's make at least one batch of hard cider.

Note- Here is a great idea for a Hard Apple Ginger Cider. About two inches of a fresh ginger root that has been peeled will work nicely. Place fresh ginger root in a food processor and pulverized it. Now add this to the cider while you're pasteurizing it. This will help in pasteurizing the ginger and in infusing the flavor of the ginger into the cider. There are several other methods like this you can use to create some rather interesting flavors of hard cider. There are no mistakes in this hobby, only lessons to be learned.

NOTES

CHAPTER FOUR
HOT SWEET APPLE CIDER RECIPES

Nothing is better during the winter season than a steaming hot mug of apple cider. The holidays wouldn't be the same without the rich aroma of mulled spiced apple cider in the air. These recipes are sure to become favorites with your friends and family.

Hot Canadian Buttered Apple Cider

Hot apple cider sweetened with maple syrup Canadian style. Topped with a delicious spiced butter, this makes one delightful drink.

Ingredients

16 ounces of apple cider

½ cup maple syrup

Spiced Butter

¼ cup butter at room temperature

¼ teaspoon allspice

¼ teaspoon nutmeg

Directions

In a saucepan over low heat, bring the apple cider and maple syrup to a simmer for 20 minutes.

In a small bowl, mix the butter with the nutmeg and allspice ensuring to mix well.

Pour hot cider into mugs and top with spiced butter mixture to taste.

Hot Strawberry Apple Cider

A sweet and delightful berry infused cider.

Ingredients

32 ounces of apple cider

1 10 ounce pack of frozen strawberries

1 cinnamon stick

½ teaspoon cloves

½ teaspoon allspice

Directions

In a saucepan over low heat, bring the apple cider, frozen strawberries, cinnamon stick and cloves to a simmer for 30 minutes. Stir occasionally.

Remove from heat and strain through a sieve with cheesecloth or a coffee filter.

Pour into mugs, sprinkle with allspice and serve.

Hot Pomegranate Apple Cider

A sweet and delightful pomegranate infused cider with brown sugar

Ingredients

32 ounces of apple cider

20 ounces pomegranate juice

4 ounces orange juice

1 cinnamon stick

8 tablespoons packed light brown sugar

½ teaspoon allspice

Directions

In a large saucepan bring the apple cider, pomegranate juice, brown sugar, orange juice, and stick cinnamon to a boil ensuring to stir the mixture. Reduce heat and allow to simmer for 10 minutes, stirring occasionally.

Remove from heat and take out the cinnamon stick and strain through a sieve. Pour into mugs, sprinkle with allspice and serve.

Hot Merry Berry Apple Cider

A sweet and delightfully infused cider with raspberries, blueberries, and strawberries

Ingredients

32 ounces of apple cider

12 ounces fresh or frozen berries, a mixture of different berries

1 cinnamon stick

4 tablespoons packed light brown sugar

Directions

In a large saucepan bring the apple cider, berries, brown sugar and stick cinnamon to a boil ensuring to stir the mixture. Reduce heat and allow to simmer for 10 minutes, stirring occasionally.

Remove from heat and take out the cinnamon stick and strain through a sieve with cheesecloth or coffee filter to remove the seeds. Pour into mugs and serve.

Hot Apple Pear Cider

A different twist to cider with the flavor of pears

Ingredients

32 ounces of apple cider

1 can of pears, 14.5 to 16 ounces with syrup

1 cinnamon stick

½ teaspoon ground ginger

½ teaspoon allspice

Directions

Take the can of pears with syrup and puree in a blender or food processor.

In a large saucepan bring the pureed pears, apple cider, ginger, allspice, and stick cinnamon to a boil ensuring to stir the mixture. Reduce heat and allow to simmer for 10 minutes, stirring occasionally.

Remove from heat and take out the cinnamon stick and strain through a sieve. Pour into mugs and serve.

Hot Mulled Apple Cider, New England Style

A traditional favorite and one that is hard to beat.

Ingredients

32 ounces of apple cider

1/3 cup packed light brown sugar

2 cinnamon sticks, ¼ teaspoon ground ginger, ¼ teaspoon cloves, ½ teaspoon allspice, and ½ teaspoon nutmeg tied up in a piece of cheesecloth.

Directions

In a large saucepan bring the apple cider and the cheesecloth bag of spices to a boil. Reduce heat and allow to simmer for 20 minutes, stirring occasionally.

Remove from heat and take out the bag of spices. Pour into mugs and serve.

Hint- If you do not have any cheesecloth available, you can use a coffee filter and string to tie it off or a tea ball.

NOTES

CHAPTER FIVE
SWEET APPLE CIDER SMOOTHIES

Smoothies are a great delicious drink that can be enjoyed anytime. Besides being a healthy drink that promotes a smooth running digestive system, delivers nutrients to your system quickly, it serves as an excellent way to beat the heat. Providing a much welcomed break from the day or for starting your day, smoothies are simply a great refreshing drink. And smoothies made with sweet apple cider offer a unique twist to this popular beverage. Enjoy the following recipes and keep the doctor away by having an apple a day, even if it is in a delightfully delicious smoothie.

Tips When Blending

There are no secrets to making a great smoothie. However there are a few tips that will make your experience more enjoyable. First, get a good blender. It's important to select a blender that can handle the job. Ensure that it has the power and is durable enough to stand up to chopping the ice for the smoothies.

The best process to use when making a smoothie is to add the liquids first. Give it a swirl to get the ice well chopped and blended. Next, add your fruits. If you are adding quite a bit of fruits and or vegetables, add a little at a time. Blend until the desired consistency.

You can adjust the thickness of your smoothie. For a thinner smoothie, add more liquid. For a thicker smoothie, you can reduce the amount of liquid or add more fruits or vegetables.

Have fun and experiment with different ingredients to create your very own recipes. There are no mistakes made, only lessons learned.

Apple Cider Smoothie with Carrot and Celery

A refreshing and healthy drink everyone will enjoy

Ingredients

8 ounces apple cider

4 ounces carrot juice or 1 large chopped carrot

1 stalk of celery

1 teaspoon lemon juice

1 cup ice (optional)

Directions

Place ingredients in a blender or food processor and puree mixture. Pour and serve.

Mango Banana Apple Cider Smoothie

A refreshing and healthy drink for fans of mangoes and bananas

Ingredients

8 ounces apple cider

1 banana

1 mango, peeled and sliced

1 teaspoon lemon juice

1 cup ice (optional)

Directions

Place ingredients in a blender or food processor and puree mixture. Pour and serve.

Coconut Apple Cider Smoothie

A refreshing and healthy drink with the sweet taste of coconut that everyone will enjoy

Ingredients

8 ounces apple cider

8 ounces coconut milk

1 banana

½ teaspoon nutmeg

1 cup ice (optional)

Directions

Place ingredients in a blender or food processor and puree mixture. Pour and serve.

Apple Cider with Yogurt Smoothie

A frothy and refreshing drink everyone will enjoy frothy

Ingredients

8 ounces apple cider

8 ounces low-fat vanilla yogurt

½ of a banana

2 tablespoons blue agave syrup (optional)

½ cup ice (optional)

Directions

Place ingredients in a blender or food processor and puree mixture. Pour and serve.

Creamed Apple Cider Smoothie

This is an indulgence that begs to be experienced

Ingredients

8 ounces apple cider

1 banana

1 cup heavy whipping cream

½ teaspoon apple pie spice (optional)

½ cup ice (optional)

Directions

Place ingredients in a blender or food processor and puree mixture. Pour and serve.

Apple Cider with Strawberries and Banana Smoothie

A refreshing and sweet drink everyone will enjoy

Ingredients

8 ounces apple cider

8 ounces fresh strawberries, (you may use frozen)

1 banana

½ cup ice (optional)

Directions

Place ingredients in a blender or food processor and puree mixture. Pour and serve.

Creamed Apple Cider with Strawberries and Banana Smoothie

A decadently delicious drink.

Ingredients

8 ounces apple cider

8 ounces fresh strawberries, (you may use frozen)

1 banana

8 ounces premium vanilla ice cream

Directions

Place ingredients in a blender or food processor and puree mixture. Pour and serve.

Peach Apple Cider Smoothie

Sure to be a summertime favorite

Ingredients

8 ounces apple cider

8 ounces fresh peaches, peeled, pitted, and sliced, (canned or frozen can be used as a substitute)

½ cup ice or plain yogurt (optional)

Directions

Place ingredients in a blender or food processor and puree mixture. Pour and serve.

Apricot Apple Cider Smoothie

Ah, apricots and apples. Does it get any better than this?

Ingredients

8 ounces apple cider

8 ounces fresh apricots, peeled, pitted and sliced, (you may use frozen or canned)

½ cup ice or plain yogurt (optional)

Directions

Place ingredients in a blender or food processor and puree mixture. Pour and serve.

The Power Packed Apple Cider Smoothie

A refreshing green drink packed with good stuff

Ingredients

16 ounces apple cider

1 cup spinach

1 cup parsley

1 cup kale

2 Kiwis, peeled and sliced

½ cup ice (optional)

Directions

Place ingredients in a blender or food processor and puree mixture. Pour and serve.

A Plum Good Apple Cider Smoothie

This one is, well, just plum good

Ingredients

16 ounces apple cider

8 ounces fresh plums, peeled, pitted and sliced

½ cup ice or plain yogurt (optional)

Directions

Place ingredients in a blender or food processor and puree mixture. Pour and serve.

Honeydew Apple Cider Smoothie

So sweet and delicious too

Ingredients

8 ounces apple cider

8 ounces honeydew, peeled and sliced

½ cup ice or plain yogurt (optional)

Directions

Place ingredients in a blender or food processor and puree mixture. Pour and serve.

Blueberry Grapefruit Apple Cider Smoothie

A delightful smoothie with a different twist

Ingredients

8 ounces apple cider

8 ounces fresh blueberries (you may use frozen)

4 ounces fresh squeezed grapefruit juice

½ cup ice (optional)

Directions

Place ingredients in a blender or food processor and puree mixture. Pour and serve.

Orange Apple Cider Smoothie

A refreshing favorite after a long day in the sun

Ingredients

8 ounces apple cider

4 ounces fresh squeezed orange juice, (you may use frozen)

½ cup ice or plain yogurt (optional)

Directions

Place ingredients in a blender or food processor and puree mixture. Pour and serve.

"The Dreamsicle" Orange Apple Cider Smoothie

This is the cat's meow

Ingredients

8 ounces apple cider

4 ounces fresh squeezed orange juice, (you may use frozen)

1 cup premium vanilla ice cream

Directions

Place ingredients in a blender or food processor and puree mixture. Pour and serve.

NOTES

CHAPTER SIX
COLD SWEET APPLE CIDER DRINKS

Shake things up with these exciting recipes for using sweet apple cider in a variety of punches and drinks. These recipes are designed for one to two servings however, simply increase the proportions to meet your needs. Feel free to play around with different juices in creating your own concoctions of delightful drinks. And when the weather turns cold, try them as a hot drink. Either way, these recipes are sure to please.

Ginger Apple Cider Punch

A summertime favorite

Ingredients

16 ounces apple cider

16 ounces ginger ale

8 ounces fresh squeezed orange juice (frozen may be used)

Directions

Pour the ingredients into a pitcher and stir. Chill and serve or serve over ice

Tahiti Time Apple Cider Punch

Another summertime favorite

Ingredients

16 ounces apple cider

8 ounces pineapple juice

8 ounces fresh squeezed orange juice (frozen may be used)

8 ounces mango juice

Directions

Pour the ingredients into a pitcher and stir. Chill and serve or serve over ice

Cranberry Apple Cider Punch

Cranberry delicious

Ingredients

16 ounces apple cider

8 ounces cranberry juice (bottled or frozen)

Directions

Pour the ingredients into a pitcher and stir. Chill and serve or serve over ice

White Grape Apple Cider Punch

A light and sweet drink

Ingredients

16 ounces apple cider

16 ounces white grape juice

Directions

Pour the ingredients into a pitcher and stir. Chill and serve or serve over ice

Pomegranate Apple Cider Punch

Pomegranate delicious

Ingredients

12 ounces apple cider

12 ounces pomegranate juice

4 ounces orange juice

Directions

Pour the ingredients into a pitcher and stir. Chill and serve or serve over ice

Sparkling Spiced Apple Cider Punch

Pomegranate delicious

Ingredients

12 ounces apple cider

12 ounces ginger ale

1 teaspoon allspice

Cinnamon sticks

Lemon twist

Directions

Pour the ingredients into a pitcher and stir. Chill and serve or serve over ice. Use cinnamon sticks and lemon twist as a garnish

Sparkling Spiced Blood Orange Apple Cider Punch

Pomegranate delicious

Ingredients

12 ounces apple cider

12 ounces sparkling blood orange soda

½ teaspoon allspice

½ teaspoon ground ginger

Cinnamon sticks

Lemon slices

Orange slices

Directions

Pour the ingredients into a pitcher and stir. Chill and serve or serve over ice. Use cinnamon sticks, lemon and orange slices as a garnish

CHAPTER SEVEN
OTHER TEXAS JACK RECIPE BOOKS

Texas Jack's Famous Caramels Secret Recipe Book

ASIN: B00FIHQ1CQ

This recipe book has a total of 21+ recipes focusing on Texas Jack's Famous Caramels. What makes this recipe book different is it is easy to follow and understand. Including a wide variety of over 14 caramel recipes from Traditional caramels to Pumpkin Spice caramel, Bourbon Chocolate caramel to the crazy delicious Wild Turkey with Honey caramel, these are sure to please everyone. There are also 4 Fudge recipes including the "Andes" Chocolate Mint Fudge and a "Fast and Simple" Fudge with only two ingredients that is so easy to make, you'll be making this one right away.

Along with the caramel and fudge recipes, there is a recipe on how to make the "Fruteria" series of Texas Jack's Famous Pralines. The recipes for these pralines incorporate the use of dried fruits like Mango, Papaya, Cantaloupe, Pineapple or Dates to create a delightful new twist on an old southern favorite. Also included is a recipe for Pumpkin Spice and Apple Spice Pecan Pralines, sure to be a Holiday Favorites this year.

Texas Jack's Famous Pralines Secret Recipe Book

ASIN: B00BLOPWV6

A Praline is a Sweet Southern Treat made up of sugar, cream, vanilla extract, and pecans that can be compared to fudge. This treat is famous throughout the South and over the years, there have been many variations of pralines made. The praline recipes in this book are easy to follow and easier to make using everything from chocolate, coconut, macadamia nuts, almonds, ginger, Amaretto, to Spice Rum.

This is a recipe book containing 12 great different recipes for making Pralines that you can change to make them your own by replacing the flavorings and nuts to whatever suits your fancy. There are also 4 cookie recipes, 4 fudge recipes, and a recipe for making Aunt Bill's Brown Candy and if you have never had Aunt Bill's Brown Candy, well, you aint living, so here is the recipe and get busy living!

Included in this book is the recipe for the all-time favorite, Texas Jack's Calico Cookies. These will leave a smile on your face and a sure bet to please any company that might come calling, so get back to better simpler times and enjoy some Old Fashion Southern Treats!

Texas Jack's Famous Sweet Potato Recipes

ASIN: B00GM11FJQ

This edition focuses on a Southern favorite, the sweet potato. There are over 25 different recipes including recipes for pies, casseroles, mash, hash, cupcakes, even a sweet potato cornbread and biscuits. With easy to follow recipes, this will become a "go to" book for the chef desiring to create a wonderful dessert using sweet potatoes.

Yummy and Sweet Potatoes go together like peas and carrots. This is a vegetable that can be utilized all year long to create some of the most delightfully delicious desserts that you have ever had. Have some fun and cook up a sweet potato dish that will sure to become a family favorite. Enjoy!

Texas Jack's Famous Christmas Pie Recipes

ASIN: B00HCZUUKQ

This edition focuses on 27 different pie recipes offering an excellent variety of choices for the holidays. From the classic Texas Jack's Brown Butter Pecan Pie to a Lemon Coconut Buttermilk Pie, there is something here for everyone. Lovers of chocolate, sweet potatoes, pumpkin, walnuts, key lime, and more will be pleased with these easy to make pies. Yummy Delicious for sure!

Texas Jack's Famous Smoothie Recipes

ASIN: B00L1BBZWE

The only limit to making smoothies is your imagination. You can make then as sweet or as tart as you want. You can make then extremely healthy or sinfully delightful. You have the ability to make your smoothie to fit the mood at the moment, the power to create whatever your heart desires.

An excellent aspect to smoothies is they are great as a breakfast drink, a dessert, or a mid-day snack. Plus the range of ingredients is boundless. There is nothing too strange that you can't use. Well, maybe. I don't think I would like an Anchovy and Sardine smoothie but that doesn't mean someone wouldn't like one. Either way, there is a recipe for that too.

However, the greatest aspect to the art of smoothies is the Health Benefits they can provide. Smoothies are an excellent source for fiber and nutrients. Drinking a healthy smoothie will provide you with a ton of good stuff for you in a most delicious way. Consuming raw fruits and vegetables helps in keeping you hydrated, providing your body with much needed fuel, and making your digestive track happy.

Well with all of that and without further ado, let's get started making some delightful and delicious smoothies.

Texas Jack's Famous "How to Infuse Vodka" Recipe Book
ASIN: B00L9I43VY

Are you tired of the same old boring drinks made with the same old flavored vodkas bought from the store? Are you looking for something new, exciting, or different? Something that will not only impress your friends and family but you too? Would you like to have your own "Signature" vodka that folks will desire? The prefect gift that they would want to have for their birthday, holidays, or any other special occasion? Then folks, this is the book for you. Texas Jack's "How to Make Infused Vodka" Recipe Book will have you on the path to making delightfully new flavors of infused vodka in no time. Yep, with this book the only limit to what you can create is your imagination. Join the Texas Jack Nation of fun food and drink today!

Infused vodkas have become very popular over the last few years. In fact, some would call it a rage within the industry. One look down the vodka aisle at any local liquor store will confirm that. From vanilla, root beer, marshmallow, to bacon, whatever you can think of, it's available at a store somewhere. Now days when you walk into a liquor store, there are entire rows dedicated to all the flavored vodkas produced by the leading makers of quality vodka. Some of these infused vodkas sell for a pretty penny too.

Well, good old Texas Jack has some great news for you. There is no need to buy these infused vodkas at the store. No sir. Infused vodkas are incredibly simple to make, even if you have no cooking skills. Doesn't matter if you don't know the difference between an egg flipper and a whisk, you'll be making your own infused vodka in no time. They are simple and relatively affordable to make. The only limit to creating your very own exotic flavors is your imagination.

Texas Jack's "How to Make Infused Vodka" Recipe Book offers over 70 simple recipes that are easy to make including unique flavor combinations like the "Sunday Morning Coming Down" infused vodka in honor of Johnny Cash. Including recipes for fruits, vegetables, herbs, spices, candy, and more, this is one comprehensive recipe book that will keep you knee deep in flavored vodka, that's for sure.

And if you have a hankering for more, check out Texas Jack's Famous Apple Cider Recipes: (How to Make Sweet and Hard Cider. Recipes for Smoothies, Sweet Cider Punch, and Hot Sweet Cider Drinks) for some delicious sweet and hard apple cider.

CHAPTER EIGHT
A BRIEF HISTORY OF THE ORIGINAL TEXAS JACK

Now Texas Jack Vermillion was a real live Gunslinger who rode with the Earp's in the "Vendetta Ride" just like in the movie. He was One Bad Hombre for sure and certainly was a friend to Doc Holliday.

John Wilson Vermillion, known as Texas Jack Vermillion (also known as Shoot-your-eye-out-Jack) was born 1842, Russell Co. Virginia. He was the second of 12 children born to William Vermillion and Nancy Owens. When the Civil War erupted in 1861, Texas Jack joined the Confederate cavalry under the command of General J.E.B. Stuart.

After the war Texas Jack married Margaret Horton on September 6, 1865 in Sullivan Co., Tennessee. The newlyweds moved to eastern Missouri where Jack accepted the position as Territorial Marshal for the eastern section of Missouri.

A daughter was born and named Mary and a second child followed. His name is unknown. Within a few weeks of the son's birth and while Jack was away from the home a diphtheria epidemic rambled across eastern Missouri killing Margaret and the children.

It has been written that grief stricken, Jack moved west. He surfaced in Dodge City, Kansas were he drank heavily, gambled frequently thus gaining a reputation as a " devil-may-care" gunslinger. It has also been written that when Dodge City burned for the first time that City Marshal and Deputy U.S. Marshal Virgil Earp rounded-up 23 men he could trust to prevent lot jumpers. One of those men was Jack Vermillion.

Family history tells a story that Jack turned up in Montana and became involved in a saloon fight. Jack wasn't doing so well until someone stepped in to help. That someone was Doc Holliday. The legend continues that many years later Jack received a trunk shipped to him from Holliday.

As portrayed in the movie **Tombstone**, it has been written that Jack killed a man who accused him of cheating at cards. Unlike the movie, the gunfight was viewed as unfair and Jack became a wanted man. It was on the wanted poster that his name first appeared as "Texas Jack" Vermillion.

Texas Jack rode with Wyatt Earp during his vendetta ride and again was with Wyatt during the Dodge City War. He was considered a crack-shot with a gun by those who knew him.

Vermillion joined up with the Soapy Smith gang in 1888 or 1889, and was involved in the Pocatello, Idaho train depot shoot-out, in which a rival gang was trying to kill Soapy. He disappeared from known gang movements, but was reportedly involved in another gunfight in 1890.

In 1911 Jack passed away quietly in his sleep. It is rumored that his last meal was a praline.

*sourced <http://captyak.tripod.com/texasjackvermillion/>

Here is another bit of history- "Texas Jack Vermillion did not accompany Virgil Earp as a member of the protective squad which escorted him to Tucson, March 20, 1882. Instead, Vermillion joined the vendetta posse March 21, 1882 in Tombstone, a day after the killing of Frank Stillwell in Tucson, thus Vermillion was not one of the 5 men indicted for Stilwell's killing. He presumably did participate in the killing of Florentino Cruz on March 22, and he had his horse shot out from under him during the fight at Iron Springs (March 24), in which "Curley Bill" Brocius was killed. Vermillion was himself not hit in that fight, but he had to be picked up by Doc Holliday after exposing himself to fire from the cowboys, while trying to retrieve the rifle wedged under his fallen horse."

*sourced -
http://en.wikipedia.org/wiki/Texas_Jack_Vermillion

ABOUT DENNIS WALLER

Dennis Waller, bestselling author, film maker and speaker, is recognized as an authority on Buddhism, Zen and the Tao Te Ching. His translation of the Tao has been a long standing best seller and is used throughout the academic world. He is only the second person to translate Nagarjuna's Tree of Wisdom into English since WL Campbell's translation in 1919.

He also is known for his series of "Texas Jack's Famous Recipe books, a collection of southern recipes that have been #1 best sellers on Amazon. From pralines, caramels, to making your own hard apple cider, the Texas Jack series has built up a strong and loyal following.

His current project, "In Search of The Kushtaka" released in April 2014 is a book offering different points of view from supporters and critics of the mythical creature, the Kushtaka, of the Tlingit People of Alaska. Covering the Tlingit and comparative mythologies along with thoughts from the science community and firsthand accounts of encounters with the Kushtaka, this book gives an enlightening look into the phenomena known as the Kushtaka.

In addition to the Kushtaka book, he has followed up with two more books on the myths of the Tlingit called, "Raven Tales" and "Otter Tales." Working with the legendary artist of Native American Art, Bob Patterson, Waller will be bringing out an illustrated guide to the world of the myths and legends of the Tlingit in late 2014.

NOTES

NOTES

NOTES

NOTES

Printed in Great Britain
by Amazon